WHITE STONE

White Stone

THE ALICE POEMS

Stephanie Bolster

SIGNAL EDITIONS IS AN IMPRINT OF VÉHICULE PRESS

Véhicule Press acknowleges the support of
The Canada Council for the Arts for its publishing program.
Although attempts have been made to contact all owners of copyrighted
material, the publisher will be pleased to acknowledge any
omissions in future editions of the book.

Signal Editions editor: Michael Harris
Cover art and design: J.W. Stewart
Photo of author: Thomas Bolster
Typeset in Perpetua by Simon Garamond
Printing: AGMV/Marquis Ltée

CANADIAN CATALOGUING IN PUBLICATION

Bolster, Stephanie
White stone : the Alice poems
(Signal editions)
ISBN 1-55065-099-8

1. Alice (Fictitious character : Carroll)—Poetry.
I. Title. II. Series.

PS8553.O479W55 1998   C811'.54   C98-900197-0
PR9199.3.B578W55 1998

Published by Véhicule Press
P.O.B. 125, Place du Parc Station
Montreal, Quebec H2W 2M9

http://www.cam.org/~vpress

Distributed by General Distribution Services

Printed in Canada on alkaline paper.

For my family

and in memory of my grandmothers,
Daisy Florence Bate Lockwood (1899-1986)
and
Catherine Alys Matthews Bolster (1909-1991)

CONTENTS

ACKNOWLEDGEMENTS

Poems in this book have appeared, usually in different forms and often under different titles, in *The Antigonish Review, The Backwater Review, Breathing Fire: Canada's New Poets* (edited by Lorna Crozier and Patrick Lane, Harbour Publishing), *The Capilano Review, The Cream City Review* (USA), *Grain, The Malahat Review, Missing Jacket, The New Quarterly, NeWest Review, Orbis* (UK), *Poetry Canada Review, Poetry Ireland Review, Prairie Fire, Qwerty, Room of One's Own* and *TickleAce.*

A much earlier version of this manuscript, entitled *Alice's Evidence,* co-won the Norma Epstein Award (University College, University of Toronto) in 1993. The poem "In Which Alice Is Born 100 Years Later" won *The Backwater Review*'s Hinterland Poetry Contest in 1997.

I am grateful to the many people whose intelligence, perceptiveness, imagination, sensitivity and severity have helped shape this manuscript. Special thanks to Christopher Patton, Barbara Nickel, Keith Maillard, George McWhirter, Caroline Davis Goodwin, the University of British Columbia's advanced poetry workshop (1992/93), Don Coles, Rhea Tregebov, Diana Brebner and Michael Harris. Thanks also to the University of B.C.'s Department of Creative Writing and the Graduate Fellowship fund, B.C. Cultural Services, the Writers' Development Trust and the Banff Centre. Most importantly, thank you to my family and Patrick Leroux, for believing in me.

WHOSE EYES

[in which we look upon Alice's childhood]

DARK ROOM

We're here, the three of us, lit by one candle.
Dodgson's wrist dips into solutions;
he nudges a glass plate to make her be there

sooner. Standing on a box, Alice peers down—
when will she appear in the slow mirror
that is not a mirror? A flame wavers, kept far away

so it won't burn, kept small so it won't ruin her
development. Two faces wait above the vat
where Alice will loom little, stopped.

But not: already hair has fallen in her eyes.
He tucks it back behind her ear, flourishes
the cleaner of his hands. *Now?* she asks.

She tugs his cuff. They don't seem to know
I'm here, poet on the corner stool, watching
a kind of homecoming. As a child I reached

to shift myself in chemicals, wanting my image
perfect in that reddish light and tang.
But the me who darkened with such grace

was ordinary once appeared, and stayed
that way. Alice gasps as she comes into view.
He hands the bathed girl to her, dripping,

says she's lovely in those rags. She laughs—
then looks a long time at her beggar self.
Although it's dim, I think I can say with near

assurance he does not attempt
to unlatch her collar. It's time for tea.
He draws back the curtain and she leaves,

he follows. This room is long and narrow, full
of longing. Outside, cups clink. Here I steep,
emulsified. Her milky shoulders start to dry.

APERTURE, 1856

First the flood of chemicals:
guncotton, ether, silver
nitrate. Then forty-five long seconds
of stillness—and she only three
and quick. Did they meet because

of a raising of eyebrows, curiouser
about each other than about anyone
else in the garden? Her sisters
blurred into foliage;
he smelled of medicine. He was

twenty-four, did not choose her
as his favourite until the *Adventures*
six years later. But something began
that afternoon, marked in his diary
"with a white stone."

Her blue eyes tight buds.
Her mousy thatch straight across
the forehead. Spring everywhere threatening
to open them both: tense in that unfurling
garden, during the long exposure.

After his first meeting with Alice Liddell on 25 April 1856, Charles Dodgson wrote in
his diary, "I mark this day with a white stone." The expression originates in Catullus'
"*Lapide candidiore diem notare*," (Poem 68, line 148) which translates as "to mark with an
especially white stone the (lucky) day." The English version was quite commonly used in
Victorian times.

WHOSE EYES

Perhaps he named that desirous stillness
he required not posing but hinting. Perhaps
he called the game Pretend—*you want something
very badly, but someone will not give it to you,
though there is a small chance they might.*
As he tilted her head down she may have thought
of pink iced cakes reserved for guests, gazed at them
from under shadowed lids as he murmured, *There.*

You are just right. To this Oxford don
with that huge contraption of a camera
and a large nose, this quiet man with waves in his hair,
she may have given these looks to be his characters.
Pretend you are the Queen of Hearts, in a huff—
and at once she found the feeling that would make
the face: her servants bustled to paint white roses
red, flamingoes bent into croquet mallets at her wish.

Nestled close against the lens, the dark
cloth draped over his head, did he not yearn
to crawl into the tunnel of the aperture?
He might have found that place where she
waited with her long-lashed eyes, clear
in black and white, just a breath away,
while the little girl had already flounced outside
to play hide and seek in the red garden.

SYMBOLIC LOGIC

It was no accident that Dodgson
was a mathematician, knew the measures
of a narrow waist, slender wrists, a flowered
mouth that always asked for more.
He exchanged stories for these—a tale
of a swim in a teary puddle
for her smile, the zero
of her missing tooth.

Nor was his study of symbolic logic
a tangential pursuit, the proving
of inevitabilities simple as the rules
of a game, *this* yields *that*, like baking bread.

The only difficulty: that she
infected his symbols, her breasts
the figure of an 8 turned
sideways, rising infinitely slowly.

When he published *Looking-Glass*,
Alice was nineteen and wore her hair up;
from his last forced portrait she regarded him
with sullen adult eyes. He sent her
the first copy bound in goatskin and never
heard a thank you, retreated into numbers
now turned unfaithful, calculations
always yielding those hourglass 8's.

Her framed childhood
photo on his desk, *The Beggar Maid*,
her skin grown yellow with its age, her chest
a Euclidean plane.

PORTRAIT OF DODGSON AS *THE BEGGAR MAID*

Imagine *his* hand reaching out.
His pallid chest with ribs

to count upon: this Alice, that
Ellen Terry, another the little

girl down the lane. But wait:
he's still a child, and all the other

boys at Rugby have torn
his uniform to bits. *N-n-no*,

his stammer they mimic, call him
a muff, stone him until he begs

they go. Alone in the open
he remembers his sister's

upturned eyes, innocent
of this. She would not hurt

a mouse. She would not know
him now. As rain collects

in his cupped hand, drains
through, he prays she will stay

holy as all well-bred maids
still young enough to save him.

WHITE STONE

Those words in their clean, even hand
transformed a page into a promise.
He must have read them daily
till they seemed to form a stone's round
gleam, its small but certain heft—

the diary's pages opened of their own accord
as though there *were* a stone kept there.

Or some round thing: it might increase
to harvest moon, compress to diamond
ring. It was a shining shape

receding as he neared it. For seven years
he sought to make it real, and his alone,

until Dean Liddell's wife suspected his intent
and stepped on it. It was not stone at all—

a shell lay smashed and hollow
in his hands. He let the pieces fall

between the pages of the latest volume
where they lodged for decades, shelved.

Long past his death marked on a slab,
his niece found fragments broken
in a book and tore those pages loose.

Today the volume opens to the absence
of own accord as though there were

a stone kept there. We seek
to measure it according to our own
desire, test its substance, hold it
to the light to see what lives inside.
It is a shining shape receding as we near it.

THE CURSE, 1863

That night her insides might have clenched:
blood stains through her underclothes
while she tosses in white sheets.
Then at dawn a word, *breach*,
whispered through the walls
as Miss Prickett wipes her clean for church.

Alice asks if this word describes her sickness,
if the servants are concerned, but Miss Prickett says
it's nothing of the sort, just "the curse,"
quite normal. It's merely growing up.

But *breach* describes the feel of it,
as if a leech has sucked her dry and white.
The mirror shows her someone else.

Mr. Dodgson, who loves pink cheeks,
doesn't come to take her picture, doesn't
send a note with kisses and a riddle to explain.
Her parents shush her questions
in the sitting room with boring guests; Miss Prickett
leads her to her room and shuts the door.

Thighs pressed to stop her insides coming out,
Alice steals off, scrapes her name
in Father's marble desktop, knocks ink
over his Greek scribbles. She taints
Mother's perfume with vinegar,
chews loose the stitches of her own best dress,
pummels Old Pricks for catching her,
for her droning tales of ordinary
tea-parties and dumb rabbits.

This must be all her ears are worthy of.
No more his spun adventures, that twitch
in his lips as he said her name.
Alice, who are you now?

THAMES

The ongoing story has briefly paused.
Three Liddell girls fidget as Dodgson gazes
at rushes edging the banks, oaks bending over them.

Please! Alice squeezes from her throat and he's back
in the story: a small doorway, a garden.
Her mouth opens, each distant lily nodding to her gaze,

but he says she's too tall to get in and her lips clamp shut.
He knows she's too young to be kept out of gardens.
He's gone too far, he's lost. As he drifts, searching,

words swim up through him toward her waiting eyes:
Alice fell, *Alice found*, *Alice cried*. Her foot just an inch
from his, her sisters nestled there alike as eggs in cups.

And me: where do I fit? Do I sit on that bank a hundred
years beyond his reach; am I the fish that flits as Alice
dips her oar? I am her eyes that shy from his

and look again when he can't see; I watch
his halting mouth and think *how smart he is, how big,*
how funny that this man likes me. I am his need

to make a story good enough to hold her
like no photograph, his hope that her foot will stay close
and his knowledge that it won't; her fear that he'll

stop the tale now or that it will not end,
ever. On that river, my pole lodges in stones and I
lose my grip. My punt slips away with me on it.

No one notices. The river flows only one way—
away. Sick for home but too old to admit it,
I watch the oaks they watched. I am hours on that river

hovering above myself, too close, not close enough.

CLOSE YOUR EYES AND
THINK OF ENGLAND

[in which we consider Alice's adulthood]

IN WHICH ALICE POSES FOR
JULIA MARGARET CAMERON, 1872

Cordelia

"What shall Cordelia speak? Love, and be silent."

—King Lear

What father has your honesty
betrayed? Your own brooked
no favourites but Dodgson made you
his. You offered love: unspeaking,

true, but not the sort he sought.
According to your bond
you walked with him awhile and then
you stopped. Now grown, and still

he sends you books in which
the face of your unfurrowed girlhood
drifts. What prince will take you now,
mock Queen of an old man's kingdom?

He who made you his beloved
has hung your coy and tattered
likeness in his private chambers.
Had you not become a still life

in his darkroom, you would not be
here now, waiting for another lens
to take you in and make a new
self, neither you nor Alice.

Pomona

"Pomona was the Roman divinity of the trees....often represented with fruits in her bosom and a pruning knife in her hand."
—Mike Weaver, *Julia Margaret Cameron 1815-1879*

What use in posing as a goddess
who would not be seduced—
when there's no danger of seduction
now? Not all beloved girls grow up

to beauty. Your hair's brittle
as last year's nests; only your name
is worth a second glance.
Just as Dodgson guessed

you craved some magic,
and turned your hope into pretend
desire, this woman with a camera
tries to make a mythic

bearing out of your frustration.
It will not work. You'll look
a witch, your power gone
all wrong. No man will come.

The photographs will stop.
You're done: a replica
at twenty-one. Like him
you've grown too old too young.

St. Agnes

"St. Agnes, martyred...at the age of thirteen, is the patron saint of virgins. Legend has it that if a virtuous young girl performs the proper ritual, she will dream of her future husband on the evening before St. Agnes' Day, which falls on January 21."
—*The Norton Anthology of English Literature*

Why, having slept with upward
gaze and hunger every Eve
hoping to be shown your future
husband, must you now be her?

A cruel trick to press this crown
into your head, wed you in white
to God alone. You've had enough
of distant men—you want to be

not Alice but a woman, waist
unlatched. Each Eve your sleep
is blank. Each morning after, your face
inside a frosted mirror no man glances into.

Today the shutter's snapped you in.
Through a hole you see a light, a girl
in white. Is this your dream?
She cannot be the answer.

IN WHICH THE POET'S GRADUATION
PHOTOGRAPH IS TAKEN

A poet, the photographer muses
when I confess, *interesting. What will you
do?* While he squints at the lens—
twisting a little me from blurred
to clear—I hold a fabric rose.

I've spent four years folded in books;
now I've fallen in this burrow
lined with badly-painted backdrops,
where a man will take me
in his choice of poses and will not wholly

let me go. One summer I walked
by a lake, past a stranger who marked me
with his eyes and remarked: *You will not
have a happy life.* What in me
made me believe him? *Look, here,*

the photographer says, *where my hand is.
Pretend you see your future
here.* I turn to where the shadow
of his gesture seeps along the wall.
A little door appears. I have no key.

There, he breathes, as sweat runs
down my side beneath the borrowed robe.
Your future, he repeats, his finger
poised to click me permanently
here, *why aren't you smiling?*

IN WHICH ALICE IS IN LOVE WITH
QUEEN VICTORIA'S YOUNGEST SON, 1873

Somewhere under her vast skirts, Victoria
put down her foot. Your mother followed suit.
And you, Children of Victoria, you cloaked
carved legs of furniture to save yourselves
the bother of the body. Against all rules
Prince Leopold's blood ran. His mother
praised him as a fine bruised grape.

You were too common for his haemophilia.
So small your tightly-woven bones,
you were the girl fat women yelled at.
Your head would have to go. Be hands
to hold aloft a cup of tea, be waist.
Don't call them all a pack of cards or they'll stomp
heel to spade, dig a hole and force you into it.

AFTER THE WEDDING, 1880

You measure the distance of your husband's sleep, watch his eyes twitch under their lids as he plays cricket in a field wide with fresh-cut grass. You would like to tell him of the one you were, how others deemed the prince you loved too pure to mingle with your blood. How you wish he had turned mute in his grief and become a pair of hands that gathered from your brush all remnants of your hair to make some keepsake ornament, as Dodgson must have framed that strand you mailed him as a child. He sent a Christ Church watercolour for your wedding at Westminster Abbey, site of royal marriages and funerals. From the prince: good wishes, a pearl horseshoe brooch.

There is nothing you can utter to the recess of Reginald's ear. Your heart beats. You chose this. Your mother nodded as you said your vows and, under paper showers, tossed your smiles. Somewhere the cake's becoming dry and hard under iced red roses.

In this bed you cannot lie. Best to watch him at his matches and applaud, best to hope to bear a child so your love will have somewhere to aim for. You cannot even ask who wrote you into this, who dropped that stone into your wedding glass of wine. You raised it, drank it down.

PORTRAIT OF ALICE AS VICTORIA'S UNIVERSE

Though she believes her subjects see her
enthroned each night in hot, insistent stars

it's you they truly worship: willowy in corsets,
abundant hair reined in, those cakes

your servants bake, ice, serve to gathered
gentry. That you, walking out a step or two

to see guests off, would not recognize yourself
alight on high only proves humility

is luminous. If a boy once wished for sixty
thousand volumes of *Alice's Adventures*,

Victoria must wish for sixty million women
with your art for watercolours, decorating

doors: women practical and sturdy,
but drawn to windows showing moon.

Her sun never goes down. Tonight your
outline of lights, cloaked in comely smog,

is so dim a sneeze from her would gust
shut your door, your light out.

ANOTHER SON, 1887

Too late, he's here, you can't
shove him back but must go on
with this gape where the core of you

should be, black hole, tunnel
you want to crawl into. Your
innards spewed into a bowl.

What you have given, these
years: three sons churned
like butter in your guts, first

Alan, then Leopold Reginald,
such heavy names you call him Rex.
This one will be Caryl, an ordinary

name you'll say, no reference
to that man who may have loved you
more than any other. He would not

love you now, your hair a barren
nest of sweat, that spattered red, steely
stink of afterbirth. He would have

turned away; he did. Somewhere inside
that girl still waits. You cup your palm
around the slackened flesh your new son left.

ALICE'S DOOR, 1890

Hands gloved against your chisel's
bevelled end, you hack at a slab
of oak until a woman roughly forms.

Now you engrave a halo,
sand the boat in which she bends,
adrift. No prince or Camelot approaches.

What curse or blessing comes upon
your version of Saint Frideswide,
Oxford's patron, whose story

has been told to you since childhood?
To avoid an avid suitor, she hid
in a barn of pigs, whose stink

concealed her from his hands.
When you recall her in a width
of wood, your fingers intuiting

a loss within those years of rings
that waver like flat water
spreading from a fallen stone,

you learn how a body is shaped
by what is taken from it.
Your plane pares hardness loose

to curls, your youngest son's,
smelling of forests and new canoes.
That woman on the river isn't you.

When the door is bolted in,
it will make a new room.
You will turn the knob and open.

TWO DEATHS IN JANUARY, 1898

Those flowers you sent to Dodgson's funeral
took your place in the crowd. Beside his stone
a perfumed heap of lilies and gentleness
of babies' breath, your name on the white card
still a child's. You spared mourners
your real face: fallen, etched with lines.

At Father's service you wore black as required,
let tears roll serenely down your cheeks, let
Reginald's husbandly elbow hook around your own.
Condolences blurred to the letter o, hollow
disbelief, *so sorry—and this on top of
the other*. You nodded at appropriate times.

For months your griefs brushed past each other,
draped and faceless as the men who left them.
On a wall inside the Deanery appeared a spreading
damp the servants covered with a chair
and wouldn't let you see. It seemed the profile of a man.

Then one morning, alone in your husband's unused
study, you found in a whiff of ink the word *father*
and your ears buzzed, stars spun you

into darkness. Your orphaned body rocked
as on a boat down a river one ancient, golden
afternoon, but no one to tell the stories, no one to row.

CLOSE YOUR EYES AND THINK OF ENGLAND

Did you follow that advice
while your husband strained for sons?
Or only once the eldest two were dead

in the Great War, and you guessed
what sodden nights had all along
been for? Your country is no mother.

Your children's country was in books,
a small and tangled patch

Dodgson planted years before—
your hand hazy in warm green water,
his words like dragonflies by your ear.

His words the children who lived
beyond all expectation. Your sons

lie broken underneath a land of stones
and bones and mud. England recovers,
Wonderland flourishes. Alice keeps on

cheating: she closes her eyes,
goes underground, comes back.

IN WHICH THE POET AND ALICE
ARE SUDDENLY OLD

Side by side in our chairs, we are two bent women
at a leaded window. It's overcast. I take notes
as you intone your catalogue of loss, sons and sister
gone, husband, love, who's left? I reach

for your wrist but you tear yourself from me,
cry *Go away,* as though I've backed you
into this corner. Did you dream me old
to cure your loneliness or have you become

the grandmothers I didn't sit beside as they died?
I was young, a hundred years beyond you,
and let myself fall from full colour into
monochrome. We're grey with loss of childhood,

we make believe it was all perfect then.
Remember, you begin—and all shimmers to a bit of sun.
To not foresee: that lack was what we had, and lost
as we enlarged beyond our photographs.

You still believe a shutter-click will reunite you
with yourself. I take my camera out. But, my aged
mind elsewhere, I leave the lens cap on:
aim at you and photograph a blackness absolute.

IN WHICH ALICE RECEIVES AN HONORARY DOCTORATE FROM COLUMBIA UNIVERSITY, 1932

The Waldorf-Astoria can't match old York Minister's restraint and manageable grandeur. Amidst these towers you've shrunk to mere inches, the height of your ankle in England. "Woman with famous name becomes grasshopper." Your giant son won't laugh at your quips but clarifies the spelling of his name—not Carroll—for reporters. Flashes capture you. But that ancient face in a crease between columns of praise cannot be yours. It's Alice whom they wish to set a square black cap upon, a girl.

And yet you're here: crowned, tassel dangling before one eye. The rising crowd becomes a field of tiger lilies mocking your white petals. *You are old,* they chant. Again he's done it, set your place at a tea party too large and empty to include you. You're here at one end of the table, and far across its length—wavering like that Atlantic you heaved your way across—she sits, a child, in England. *Hello, my dear*, you call. She's looking elsewhere, at him in those white gloves behind his tripod. She's beautiful—you never knew. You'd forgotten her open eyes, remembered only the shut Alice in books.

Hands clap somewhere. A professor stands to analyze the Alice texts as allegory. Too late—the girl is gone. Poor little Alice, her empty chair. Caryl passes you a handkerchief. You are his mother. He believes you happy at last.

DEATH, 1934

Sad, how small, tenacious,
grey you've become.

What was that mouse
slipped under the door?

The world over, we will try
to catch her into cages, snap

her vertebrae with metal,
wring her guts with poison

and fail. The papers will say
Alice in Wonderland

has passed away,
as though you were

that Alice and gone.

PORTRAITS OF ALICE, ANNOTATED

[in which she is buried and written upon extensively]

PORTRAIT OF ALICE AS CHRYSALIS

Tell her story from the caterpillar's
point of view and movement would be
slower, measured in inches, the length
of that tea table lasting for days.

We would see Alice, her stubby,
shrunken arrival at the mushroom site,
buckles and patent shoes creased
as she peered up to meet

the caterpillar's gaze, light glinting
off the top of her head, her eyes
guarded against too much curiosity.
She would never devour; only sip, nibble.

But Alice's "tomorrow" and the caterpillar's
would each be portrayed
as a Turner painting, vague and stormy,
with a light in the distance. It could be

an oncoming train, or sun
breaking open a chrysalis, or the end
of the tunnel. It could be a girl's mouth
smiling when she'd really rather not.

PORTRAIT OF ALICE AS HER OWN FOOT

"Alice's Right Foot, Esq.,
    Hearthrug,
        near the Fender.
            (with Alice's love)."
                    —Alice's Adventures in Wonderland

When Alice was huge, she wrote those words
to that foot, far down but large as a canoe
or the Deanery glimpsed from Tom Tower:
the shoe heavy and scuffed and nothing
to do with her. She made sure to mention

love, so the foot would know she remembered
their earlier attachment. She addressed it properly,
so it would not be offended and take off somewhere
she wished it not to go. In fact she was not sure
it was the right foot after all, but it might
be hurt if she expressed doubt.

As if sensible to her confusion, those words
she'd written changed upon the paper.
Like fireworks they blew apart, scalding syllables
into her sight. Even *foot* was *fo* and *ot*,
an enemy that scolded her. What wrong
had she done? Through her tears those bits of words
turned backwards——*to* and *of*——and became

the foot's letters to her, proclaiming their bond.
She told the foot, *move*, and it did,
like an old friend tapping messages in Morse.
Perhaps it heard *love* instead.

PORTRAIT OF ALICE, ANNOTATED

Who was it strung these footnotes
from her toes and scribbled
italics on her wrists, indicating perhaps
that only slim-wristed girls
were allowed to enter Wonderland?

They wound her with measuring tape,
noted the resulting data on her skin, figures
for chest and waist identical. To her mouth
was taped a parchment proclamation
detailing origins of those words she spoke

as if they were as intimately hers
as earlobes. But the evidence proved
those words had a long history of their own,
belonged to themselves and would
outlive her. Whatever she had said

to end up in this predicament
was not her fault, she was exempt, thus safe.
What could be done to her now? Even her breasts
were claimed before they'd risen; some said
he'd placed his nitrate-ridden hands there.

The critics overwrote each other
till all their words were tattooed black
upon her. *Have mercy*, she cried as they came
with the thousand-volumed weight of archives,
but those words were not hers either.

PORTRAIT OF THE POET, ANNOTATED

This woman who spent two years learning
name and tone of muscle can't believe
the tightness of my lower back. Note:

this must be what is meant by highly-
strung. Alice's back, better bred, would have
spread generously, resonant as the cello

I wish would lean, mournful between
my outspread legs. Corseted, she had
that cello shape—or hourglass, a word

a younger me confused with "looking-glass"
and saw a tiny Alice falling through.
I've been wedged a long time in the sad narrows

between her and me. Now, kneaded by skilled
hands, I fall free, my back widened to a map
on which Alice is one persistent point.

PORTRAIT OF ALICE WITH PERSEPHONE

i

It is the going underground that preserves the body,
so though Persephone is ancient
and Alice long ago became antique
each could pass for sixteen.

They stand close, arms about each other's waist,
faces pressed together—halves of an apple
cut to show the star of seeds.

They stand on opposite sides of knowing,
balance each other. What Alice lacks in weight
she makes up in fear, heavy as the denser metals.

It is the going underground that gives them
this battered look—dark crescent moons beneath
the eyes, lips swollen and split at the corners.
Dirt in their scalps, at the roots.

ii

Persephone took the pomegranate seed
Hades offered, she sucked all flavour
from it, she rolled it on her tongue,
caught it in her molar's furrow.
With a fingernail she picked it loose
and swallowed it. Were those tarts

the Queen of Hearts reported stolen
made of apples? In sufficient quantities,
apple seeds are poisonous.
Were several left in?

Alice was accused but innocent,
of course, much too young for such things
as illicitness and seeds, although one might have
thought the same of Persephone.
Certainly Alice would have been tempted
by the fragrance of warm sliced apples,
the idea of something hard in there.

iii

The difference has to do with men,
with Persephone's marriage to Hades.
Alice had choices—White Knight, Mad Hatter,
Three of Spades—but pronounced them substantial
as a pack of cards. The difference

has to do with the glint tightened
around Persephone's finger,
the magenta of pomegranate
in the creases of her palm and thighs.
Alice's thighs are clean. Except for the curve
of dirt under the nails, her hands are white
as something dead, or not yet born.

iv

Single, we would say of Alice, and yet it's clear
she's not, here with the grown woman
no mirror will let her forget,
whose name echoes *destiny*. Here with her finger
slightly narrowed at its base, as if it waits

for a ring, the way the heart waits for a single
seed to slip into its chambers
and lodge there, sprout into a tendril
that makes earth of the body.

PORTRAITS OF ALICE AS BESTIARY

white rabbit

not just any colour
but all shades spun

to perfect nothing.
eyes red-rimmed, unlucky

foot snapped in a trap's
teeth. her heart

a watch still ticking.

dormouse

named not for doors
but for sleep, *elle dort*

tout le temps
in the sugar bowl.

easier than that gape
of an extra o, another entry

to be fallen through.

mouse

not a cat that got her tail, but her own
teeth that bit, dreaming of attack.

now she drags the fear
behind her, a long and sad ending.

she cannot sleep for the hiss
of her breath and for who she'll become

out of the corner of her eye.

cheshire cat

she comes from that place
where what doesn't stay

goes——the sardine's flesh,
the other sock. she naps

on the missing crescent
of a near-full moon and smiles

at what no other eyes see.

PORTRAIT OF ALICE WITH ELVIS

Queen and King, they rule side by side
in golden thrones above the clouds.
Her giggle and wide eyes remind him
of his first young wife, and his twang
never ceases to thrill her, so different
from the prim accents of men she's known.

She sings for him, "Hound Dog"
and "Heartbreak Hotel," and he turns
the Mock Turtle's song of beautiful soup
campier with each performance, hip-twists
till her eyes stream and she melts with laughter.

Sometimes they leave their airy realm
to share a strawberry shake at Burger King
in Memphis, visit the Tate Gallery in London
solemnly to ponder the Lady of Shalott
alone and adrift in her rowboat.

In rare arguments over fame, he cites
the Churches of Elvis, the Vegas tributes,
while she mentions the Alice shop in Oxford,
the Alice ride at Disneyland. He says more books
have been written about him, but she insists hers
are of higher calibre, her words are quoted
much more often than his. He calls up wax figures,
she teapots and tarot cards. Both delight
in their limited edition collector's plates.

For dinner they fry chicken, make tea and scones,
tarts filled with peanut butter.
He runs her a lavender bubble bath,
washes her hair, greases his own.

She lays her head against his chest
during late night TV, murmurs of the man
who gave her fame, and he of the woman for whom
he won his. She wants to sway
to the beat of his heart in her ear, slow
as "Are You Lonesome Tonight." In sleep
their tear-blotched faces could be anyone's.

PORTRAIT OF ALICE WITH CHRISTOPHER ROBIN

In the midst of a winter wood
she walks like old age,
bent under falling snow and the ghost
of her written self, heavy
as bundled kindling on her back.

At a tree's base he huddles his narrow shoulders
as if lost—his head, familiar from books,
hung forward in dangerous
chilled sleep, calves downy-haired
and goose-bumped past short pants.
An italic fall of snowflakes
various as dreams across his face.

She watches his trembling lips
mumble of yellowed bears and bluster and rain,
of being irrevocably stuck,
then presses her hand to his cheek.
His lashes flutter, he shows her
his eyes made of glaciers and pronounces her name.

To the magic flame he makes
with two rubbed sticks
she gives her pinafore and white socks,
the ribbon from her fallen hair.
He fumbles with his buttons, burns
his trousers and dirty shirt.

They point to figures in the smoke—
lumpen bear, white rabbit, honey pot,
tea cup. Naked together, they watch with ash-stung
eyes and neither blink nor shiver.

THE POET AS NINE PORTRAITS OF ALICE

i

In Grade One I weep myself
waist-deep in tears.
I don't know why.

My teacher doesn't know
what to do with me.
She sends me to another teacher, down a hallway
with its rows of closed doors.
It is a long walk,
and my dress all wet.

ii

I dream the closet door in the basement opens
into somewhere larger than the closet
when turned with the right key.
The ceiling is one hundred times my height.
The floor is marked in squares of white and black.
On the walls hang blue-eyed dolls.

iii

A man I hardly know but want
to know better forgets my name,
introduces me to his roommate as Alice,
then apologizes, laughing.
I say it doesn't matter. I laugh
harder than he does.

Across a parking lot, *Alice*
called three times. When I turn
at last, I see flowers
for someone else, carried by the roommate
who's forgotten what my real name is.

He doesn't know
that at this moment I'm not coy
or afraid enough to be Alice.

iv

Age nine, I crawl
through a yellow rabbit hole
at the Enchanted Forest theme park in Oregon.

I am wearing my Shaun Cassidy t-shirt.
He is twice my age. I am not a child.

Before sleep I dream of growing
older, kissing him.
I am one of Charlie's Angels,
my hair feathered, black.

v

I have a list of the recurrence of Alice
in my family tree. I am the first instance
of my own name. Something is amiss.

vi

The first man to call me beautiful
wears the caterpillar's manic
grin and breathes out the same
dazed smoke. We kiss by the river
within sight of luckless fishermen.

With him I find a patch of sky,
see tiny driveways bordered
with crocuses, backyards
with swingsets.

When he says goodbye I cry into the phone
for hours until he says he has
to go. I hang up first.

vii

That mirror at the end
of a long hallway still frightens me.

viii

Why Alice and not Cinderella?
a man asks me, over coffee
I asked him out for.

I think about pumpkins turned
to coaches, how small her feet were.
I answer that Alice is still
Alice even when she thinks
she's Mabel and she finds her own
way in and out of Wonderland.
He nods his head. I run my finger
up and down his hand.

ix

If I had a daughter, I would like
to name her Alice, but I would not.

PORTRAIT OF ALICE AS THE POET'S UNIVERSE

Awake one night I linked her stars
into the seated shape of a woman

I can't stop seeing: her back upright
against the curve of slats

while each next second exposes her
further. We are each a lens;

some nights the world is made of gazes
peering through me as I sit here

under her. I pretend she
understands, but she and many

of these stars are dead. Their light
is not for me and is not her.

HIDE AND SEEK

[in which Alice discovers the New World and eludes the poet]

VISITOR FROM OVERSEAS

I received an envelope from England, somewhat torn,
postage two pounds, cancellation stamped across a queen's face.
Inside brown paper, an ironmonger's plastic bag gasped
like my childhood rabbit just before it died. Unsealed,

Alice crawled out small and scraggly, arms stuck to her sides
and starved. I had no crumpets so fed her large Canadian
muffins instead, which she nibbled with admirable restraint.

Overnight while I slept she swelled, spurted in height until
I woke and found her crouched against the ceiling, learning
how to curse. I offered the entire contents of my fridge
but nothing shrank her back again, nothing until I told her

she was beautiful, her legs burnished as arbutus limbs. Curious,
she reduced herself to doorframe size, followed me to find
a land she'd never seen. There on a Pacific beach remembered:

rowing under shapely willows with a man three times her size,
who liked her little, who kept her between pages, sent her
wrapped over the Atlantic so as not to mar the idea of her
he kept under glass, scalloped like a fancy cake.

PORTRAIT OF ALICE AS MISSING PERSON

Someone has organized a search for her without consulting me. Etched in classic black and white, she appears on billboards, milk cartons. The world begins to seek her under hedges, in doghouses, outhouses, ruined towns.

I collect newspaper clippings till my closet overflows. Spaniels have been mistaken for her hair, shreds of bloody rag at roadsides for her pinafore. A man in Darwin, Australia says his yin-yang pendant is carved from her right incisor. A tabloid exclusive insists *she* lay inside Diana's coffin. Small girls cornered by video cameras appear to be her, until they flaunt their platform shoes, flash their braces, rave about the latest teenage babe, show their bullet wounds.

I'm the first to proclaim her truly found, on a New York subway platform, but before the flocks descend I repent, confess it's a trick with mirrors, a publicity stunt for my forthcoming book. *The hunt is futile*, I tell the press, but they're already rushing off to sue me. *Until we see the body*, the gathered fans say, *we won't believe she's gone*. When I pipe up that there never was a body, that Alice Liddell had bangs and brown hair and was probably not very witty, that even she can never be found, I'm branded a deconstructionist. *Based on a true story*, they chant, their emphasis on *true*.

I remember that joke about how do you know if there are elephants in your refrigerator. *Go to your kitchen*, I say, *look for her footprints in the butter*. They scatter to buy magnifying glasses. At home I peep into my fridge but light and hum are as they always are. Nothing scurries behind the jar of jam.

IN WHICH ALICE IS BORN 100 YEARS LATER

Fifteen in 1967, she listens to Sgt. Pepper for the first time in a cramped bedroom, her long hair brushing words on the red back of the album jacket: *hole, rain, dark, heart*. Mid-summer she steals away from Oxford with her heart and pounds filched from the biscuit tin, to San Francisco where there are real colours. No sludgy greys, no children's story with her name in it, set nearly in her own backyard. No memory glassed within her like a moth in a jar.

There she learns a sprawling accent, takes off her clothes in Golden Gate Park and feels her hair down her back, over her breasts, wears around her neck a daisy chain, gift of a nameless boy whose hair reaches farther than hers. And hears a woman with a sinister voice sing about a white rabbit, about eating mushrooms and the sizes of everything changing. Feels at the back of her neck those lingering terrors of tunnels and rabbits, hope of small doorways. Breaks the daisy chain, flees that park and the boy with the hair, for her room in a funky pink-iced Victorian house with cockroaches and slow, transforming air, puts on The Beatles and tries to remember that dream those notes first conjured. She'd still love to be turned on. She wonders if her parents have remembered to feed her cat.

She flips the cover to the front, a fresh flowered grave and Indian figures, the band in their brilliant glittering suits, all those faces, and now she recognizes him there in black and white, the don in the corner, tie knotted round his neck, eyes staring off into distance, or back into his head, where a small girl lives. Now John Lennon's voice sings that man's words, and she pictures herself on a river. But she has already been pictured, might even find her face there with Marilyn Monroe and Shirley Temple and that small blonde doll, all gathered to mourn this decade, its huge bloom collapsing inward already. She might find herself nostalgic in the crowd, if she's not the one they're all nostalgic for, the one whose burial has been proclaimed with flowers.

PORTRAIT OF ALICE AS SPIRIT

Once the moon cast your shadow
and you saw yourself complete,
your body defined black
on the night pavement
as if it belonged
as much as the grasses and the yews.
That was a long time ago.

Now you envy the ease
with which others cast shadows,
the cat brushing against her own
evidence of being

in the dim hallway,
the lily scrolling itself
black against the white wall.

The stone lays it shape
down with such assurance
you could weep.

PORTRAIT OF ALICE AS AN ENGLISH LANDSCAPE

At first you were a verdant
field, your hips slight
as the rise and fall of hills.

Soon you swelled,
were covered in a tight checkered dress.
The landscape divided
into a game of chess, each square set
with church steeple, oak tree, queen.
What value, an inch of you, an acre.

The world played other games
upon you, sank deep
holes into your feet, hid its trash
in the pit beneath your arm.

By the end you are that crone
it's said all women become—wizened
and wise. Cracked lake-beds
where your eyes were.

PORTRAIT OF ALICE AS HER OWN UNIVERSE

This big, you can't be photographed.
You are the subject and the aperture.

Of the advantages to death and myth,
this you have most deserved: space

enough to open out and be
the only thing. What are you—

a collection of meteors
trailing light? Their passage

so blurred we can only guess
what they were. Watch them.

Implode. In the black funnels
you will find all your variations.

STILL LIFE

I've got it too, that knack
for sitting still while inner
ticking hammers every

nerve and the universe
runs on like a white rabbit,
Alice's frantic tardy heart

invisible inside a cage
of lace. Now past the need
for poses, we let video take us

where and as we are.
If I could see her move,
know the way her sleeve

folded as she shifted her wrist
to write her name,
would it be like opening

a door into a garden?
I let her history fall shut
and move into my moving body.

Victoria's dead, this isn't
England, and Alice was never
just that taxidermied girl

through Dodgson's lens,
that woman's face looming
in my dark room.

When the camera turned
away, she ran. Since I began
to seek her, I've found

love, moved to a land
white as a page. I rarely stop
to think of her these days.

ALICE LAKE

Sad as a Loch, this place ought to have secrets winding deep. Instead I find a rumpled, dimpled woman in a bathing suit, who enters the water quick and unshivering, eases into a backstroke. She ripples the surface only briefly, keeps her mystery constrained as her arms.

I wait for something to rise from within, that dark curve in a blurred newsprint photograph that proves the mystery is real. But the movement comes wrong—rain that merely acts upon the surface—indentations, not eruptions.

Skunk cabbage skirts the shore like a dirty hem. Its yellow smell affronts the grey, the rain, those other anonymous plants, tentative and skeletal, rising from the water. Rain quavers their reflections. The plants remain themselves unmoving, roots underwater, tendrils keeping their distance.

The woman is a pair of arms reaching the other shore and I am a pair of eyes touching only their own lids and this rain.

VISITOR FROM OVERSEAS, REPRISE

Knowing me a foreigner, the Oxford bus driver
charges double from the hostel into town.
It's raining, just like home, but colder.
Oh, to be in England. My finger catches in a door,

bleeds on trinkets in "Alice's Shop." The salesman
lacks a hidden camera so stares at me and my friend,
indelicate in backpacks. This was where the sheep
counseled Alice in the story. I am here. Here

the real Alice bought barley sugar with her sisters.
I buy a thimble in her fictional image. We cross
St. Aldate's, pay £3.50 to pass the Christ Church gates.
There are Dodgson's former rooms above Tom Quad.

And there the Deanery wall. Entry to the garden
is forbidden, to preserve the privacy of present
Dean and Family. Have dandelions taken hold
inside the soggy lawn? Is that a waft of rose?

I lean against that wall of breaking stone, I am
photographed so quickly in the rain. She is
nowhere. If I'm not getting warmer here,
then where? Who did I dream I'd find?

THE OPENED DOOR

Today a ringing phone awoke me and I stumbled
through the blurry hallway to it. It was a doorknob

in my hand. I turned my wrist, the door became a mist
I walked through. I was in a winter field,

not home but the place I found each time I shut my eyes
to sleep. I was here, I was Here, the air equivalent

to that reddened temperature within my skin.
My gated chain of cells unlocked. I am not

what I expected. What do these footprints mean?
They are mine: those spaces where my weight

has pressed the snow, and the snow my
weight has pressed, and my weight, and my

thought of weight. This is fear, this is here,
this is me, I am: the doorway, opened.

BIOGRAPHICAL NOTE
ON ALICE LIDDELL

Alice Pleasance Liddell Hargreaves (1852-1934) was the daughter of the Reverend Henry George Liddell, co-writer of the famous *Greek Lexicon* and the Dean of Christ Church College, Oxford, where Charles Lutwidge Dodgson (1832-1898; also known as Lewis Carroll) was a Mathematics don. Known for his affinity for children, Dodgson befriended Alice and her sisters Lorina and Edith in the Deanery garden on 25 April 1856. During the ensuing years, he spent an increasing amount of time photographing Alice and her siblings and telling them stories. On a boating trip down the Thames on 4 July 1862, he began the tale that became *Alice's Adventures in Wonderland*.

Details of a mysterious break between Dodgson and the Liddells, which occurred the following year (Alice was eleven), were lost after his death—his niece, Menella Dodgson, removed his diary entries from the 27th to the 29th of June, 1863. The cause may have been a breach of etiquette, such as Dodgson planning to photograph the children with only the permission of their governess, Miss Prickett. It is possible that Alice's mother and Oxford gossipmongers disapproved of Dodgson's interest in Alice and her sisters, particularly her older sister Lorina, who was physically advanced for her age; he was also perceived by some to be courting Miss Prickett. It is also possible that Dodgson went so far as to suggest an interest in marrying Alice at some much later date. Recently, it has been proposed that he was in fact having an affair with Alice's mother, an unlikely prospect given Mrs. Liddell's formidable reputation (an Oxford rhyme of the 1880s went: "I am the Dean and this is Mrs. Liddell,/She plays the first, and I the second fiddle") and Dodgson's preference for the company of little girls, some of whom he photographed in the nude. Mrs. Liddell destroyed all of Dodgson's letters to Alice.

In any case, Dodgson would probably have lost contact with Alice around this time, as he typically abandoned—or, more frequently, was abandoned by— his child friends once they began to grow up. After this point, Alice's contact with Dodgson mainly involved small pleasantries and news of the Alice books. He took his final photograph of her in 1870.

In 1872, the noted photographer Julia Margaret Cameron (great-aunt of Virginia Woolf) photographed Alice, who was vacationing with her family near Cameron's home on the Isle of Wight. Three of these photographs portrayed Alice as Pomona, St. Agnes, and (with her sisters) one of King Lear's daughters. The same year, Queen Victoria's youngest son, Prince Leopold, came to study at Oxford. According to many sources, he and Alice became romantically involved, but marriage would have been forbidden by both sets of parents because of the discrepancy in social class. The prince, a haemophiliac, married in 1882, named his daughter (whom Dodgson later met) Alice, was godfather to Alice Liddell Hargreaves' son, Leopold, and died in 1884 from, according to Queen Victoria's journal, "a breaking of blood vessel in the head."

Edith, Alice's closest sister, died of peritonitis in 1876 at age twenty-one, just days after becoming engaged. This seems to have been one of the greatest traumas in Alice's life. As an adult, she is said to have always appeared sad.

On 15 September 1880, in Westminster Abbey, Alice married Reginald Hargreaves, a cricket player from a wealthy and respected family, whom most considered her intellectual inferior, and who apparently idolized her. They had three sons (Leopold, Reginald and Caryl), the first two of whom died in World War I. The Hargreaves led a leisurely life at Cuffnells, Reginald's servant-filled estate, where they entertained frequently.

Alice, a skilled painter and woodcarver, carved a vestry door for the Church of St. Frideswide in the East End of London in 1890. Her panel depicted the saint arriving in Oxford by boat. The church was bombed during World War II but the door survived and now stands in the Church of St. Frideswide, Osney.

After Reginald's death, Alice remained at Cuffnells for several years. Caryl, who had inherited the estate, spent weekends there until his marriage in 1930, of which she did not approve. In 1932, Alice, Caryl, and Alice's sister, Rhoda, visited the United States for a large celebration in which Alice received an honourary degree at Columbia University. Her first words on arriving in New York were: "How often do they dredge the river so that ships of deep draught may pass into port?" She was also curious about the ventilation shafts of the Holland Tunnel.

Alice died at The Breaches in Westerham, Kent (General Wolfe's home town) on 15 November, 1934. She left no will. Her effects amounted to £1371. Several years before her death, she wrote in a letter: "Poor little Alice, I am quite tired of that little lady, slightly ungrateful on my part, I admit."

All quotations on this page are taken from Colin Gordon's *Beyond the Looking Glass: Reflections of Alice and Her Family* (London: Hodder and Stoughton, 1982), pp. 173, 237, and 21.

SOURCES

Though I did not limit myself to the facts in writing these poems, I could not have imagined Alice without the following books:

Anne Clark's *The Real Alice: Lewis Carroll's Dream Child* (London: Michael Joseph, 1981), Colin Gordon's *Beyond the Looking Glass: Reflections of Alice and Her Family* (London: Hodder and Stoughton, 1982), Morton Cohen's *Lewis Carroll: A Biography* (New York: Alfred A. Knopf, 1995), Helmut Gernsheim's *Lewis Carroll: Photographer* (New York: Dover, 1969), Mavis Batey's *Alice's Adventures in Oxford* (Crawley, England: Pitkin, 1980), Derek Hudson's *Lewis Carroll: An Illustrated Biography* (New York: Clarkson N. Potter, 1977), Isa Bowman's *Lewis Carroll As I Knew Him* (New York: Dover, 1972), *The Diaries of Lewis Carroll*, edited by Roger Lancelyn Green (London: Cassell and Company, 1953), *Aspects of Alice: Lewis Carroll's Dreamchild as seen through the Critics' Looking-Glasses, 1865-1971*, edited by Robert Phillips (New York: Vanguard, 1971), *Lewis Carroll: Looking-Glass Letters*, selected by Thomas Hinde (London: Collins and Brown, 1991), the facsimile edition of *Alice's Adventures under Ground* (New York: Dover, 1965), Martin Gardner's *The Annotated Alice* and *More Annotated Alice* (Harmondsworth, England: Penguin, 1960; New York: Random House, 1990), Mike Weaver's *Julia Margaret Cameron, 1815-1879* (Boston: Little, Brown and Company, 1984), and advance press for Karoline Leach's *Shadows of Sin* (London: Peter Owen, 1998). Two films, Dennis Potter's documentary-fiction *DreamChild* (1985) and Jan Svankmajer's surreal animated *Alice* (1988) also provided information and inspiration.

Signal Editions Poetry Series
edited by Michael Harris